LOOKING BACK
FAMILY LIFE

JENNIFER LINES

LOOKING BACK

CLOTHES AND FASHION

FAMILY LIFE

FOOD AND SHOPS

HOLIDAYS AND PASTIMES

TRANSPORT

WORK

Series and Book Editor: Rosemary Ashley
Designer: Bruce Low

First published in 1991 by
Wayland (Publishers) Limited
61 Western Road, Hove,
East Sussex, BN3 1JD, England

© Copyright 1991 Wayland (Publishers) Limited

British Library Cataloguing in Publication Data
Lines, Jennifer
Family life
1. Great Britain. Family life 20th Century
I. Title II. Series
306.850941

ISBN 0-7502-0054-5

Typeset by Rachel Gibbs, Wayland
Printed in Italy by G. Canale & C.S.p.A., Turin
Bound in Belgium by Casterman S.A.

CONTENTS

INTRODUCTION 4
1 EARLY YEARS 6
2 THE FIRST WORLD WAR 11
3 BETWEEN THE WARS 14
4 THE SECOND WORLD WAR 19
5 A CHANGING WORLD 23
6 THE SEVENTIES ONWARDS 27
IMPORTANT DATES 30
GLOSSARY 31
BOOKS TO READ 31
INDEX 31

INTRODUCTION

Many different influences affect the way families live, including the society and culture around them, the traditions that have been handed down to them by earlier generations, the work they do, how much money they have to spend and how much free time they have to enjoy.

During this century, family life has probably changed to a greater extent and at a faster rate than in any other period in history. The sweeping developments that have taken place in science and in industry, the upheavals caused by two world wars, the changes in the law and in the attitudes of society – all these factors have played a part. For example, there have been times when millions of people were unable to get jobs and earn money, and this has meant that many families suffered great poverty. Sometimes wars have forced families apart, leaving women and children at home while the men went away to fight.

The backyards of the small slum houses of poor city dwellers in 1919.

An evening by the sitting-room fireside for a middle-class family in the late 1930s.

More recently, the attitudes of society have changed dramatically, and many things that were once frowned upon or even regarded as scandalous – including divorce and unmarried mothers – are now much more accepted. Fewer couples get married today, and about one in three marriages ends in divorce. There are now many one-parent families. Young people are more independent than previously, partly because they have more money. They do not have to accept their parents' ideas about clothes, music, entertainment and so on because a wide range of these are produced especially for them. What is more, they are often able to leave home at an earlier age.

All in all, perhaps the main effect of the changes that have occurred over the last ninety years is that families today are not bound together as tightly as they were.

By the 1980s, the TV had become the focal point in many family homes.

1 EARLY YEARS

For many people in Britain, the 'new age' of the twentieth century really began in January 1901, when King Edward VII came to the throne following the death of Queen Victoria. During Victoria's reign of 64 years, Britain had become the 'workshop of the world', and its richest nation. Factories and mills produced goods that were sold in dozens of foreign countries, especially in the colonies that made up the huge British Empire. While this made Britain wealthy, the people who worked in the factories were less fortunate.

The factory-workers' houses were very small, built close together in terraces along both sides of a narrow street. They had no electricity, bathroom or heating, apart from a coal fire in the kitchen. Not surprisingly, the warm kitchen was where a family spent most of their time together. Some houses had gas lighting, but only on the ground floor. Many did not even have a

City children often had nowhere to play apart from the streets.

A woman spins outside her home in Lancashire, in 1901.

water tap inside – water had to be collected in buckets from a shared tap out in the street. The houses were close to the factories where the people worked. In 1907 an observer wrote: 'the furnaces, the grey streets, a few public buildings, all set in a background of greyness, in a devastated landscape under a grey sky.'

Most married women stayed at home to look after their children and do the housework, and the husband was often the family's only breadwinner. Factory work was hard, dangerous, and badly paid. Many families found it difficult to manage. Somehow they had to earn enough money to pay the rent and buy food, clothing and other essentials. If there was any money left over, they might visit a music hall or

> 'I am a mother of eleven children – six girls and five boys. I was only nineteen when my first baby was born. My husband was one of the best and a good father. His earnings were £1 a week and he gave every penny to me. But after rent, heating and lighting, that only left me 11 shillings to keep the house going and provide for the children.
>
> Woman interviewed in 1913. (Paraphrased from *Maternity: Letters from Working Women*)

This family of four lived in just one room in London's Bethnal Green.

cinema, or save up for a Bank Holiday trip to the seaside. Life was harder still for people without jobs, and for those workers who fell ill or were injured at work. In these cases the family might have no money at all.

A rich woman steps from her grand country house into her car, 1906.

Factories and shops were closed on Sundays. Many workers, especially in the industrial areas of the north of England and in Welsh mining villages, spent part of their free time at church. For other workers Sunday was a day of recreation and a break in their hard working lives.

The weekly budget of the family of a railway-carriage washer with a wife and three children in 1911. He earned 21 shillings for working seven days a week. (From *Round About a Pound a Week* by Maude Pember Reeves, 1913)

	s. d.
Rent	7 – 0
Clothing club	1 – 2
Burial insurance	1 – 6
Coal and wood	1 – 7
Coke	0 – 3
Gas	0 – 10
Soap, soda	0 – 5
Matches	0 – 1
Blacklead, blacking	0 – 1
11 loaves of bread	2 – 7
Flour	0 – 5½
Meat	1 – 10
Potatoes and greens	0 – 9½
½ pound of butter	0 – 6
1 pound of jam	0 – 3
6 ounces of tea	0 – 6
2 pounds of sugar	0 – 4
1 tin of milk	0 – 4
Cocoa	0 – 4
Suet	0 – 2
	21 – 0

The factories, mines and mills provided a poor living for most of their workers. But the factory owners and those who bought and sold the goods, made a great deal of money. Their lives were much more comfortable than those of their employees. Between these two groups of people were the 'middle classes' – ranging from well-off 'professionals' or businessmen to poorer clerks and shop assistants.

Unlike the 'two-up-two-down' houses of the factory workers, the house of a wealthy middle-class family had eight, ten or even more rooms with expensive decorations, carpets and furniture. There was usually a coal fire in every room, and the house might also have electric lights and a telephone. 'Here I am, with wonders and pictures... magnificent couches and satin cushions... the beds with silk sheets and bows of pink silk ribbon...' wrote a young middle-class girl in 1903.

The middle-class family had several servants to cook, clean, garden, look after the children and generally take care of the

Wealthy families enjoying a day out on the River Thames in 1912.

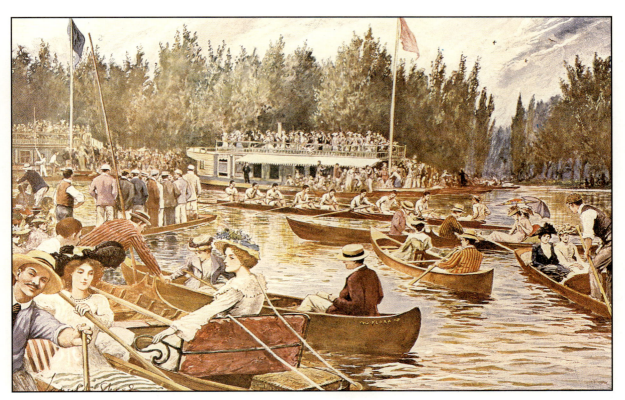

A young housemaid, supervised by the housekeeper, cleans and lays a fire in a large middle-class home. Many servants worked long, hard hours for their employers.

household. Thanks to their wealth and the labours of their servants, the family were able to enjoy plenty of leisure time. They would entertain themselves and their friends by singing songs around the piano, or they might listen to the newly invented gramophone, visit the theatre, enjoy parties, or play sports such as croquet, tennis and golf.

> 'Many of them were fashionable young women... Socially, of course, I was quite without standing among these wealthy girls... with their town addresses in Mayfair or Belgravia... My parents could not afford the... theatres and concerts to which many of them were taken... my "best" clothes were home-made and the presents that I received... did not bear comparison with the many elegant gifts that my class-mates displayed...'
>
> Vera Brittain, writing about her classmates in the early 1900s, (from *Testament of Youth*)

2 THE FIRST WORLD WAR

In August 1914, war broke out in Europe. It was to drag on for over four years. The first British troops were sent to the battlefront in France shortly after the war began. They were followed by millions of volunteers and conscripted men.

The British and their French and Belgian allies soon became bogged down in bitter fighting against the German army. Both sides dug long lines of trenches in which to shelter, and erected barbed wire fences to prevent enemy advances. Every so often, soldiers would be sent 'over the top' to attack the enemy lines and try to gain a few metres of territory. The only result of most of these attacks was hundreds or thousands of dead soldiers. As each side bombarded the other with heavy gunfire, the ground turned to thick mud.

A poster from the First World War.

'From the morning of September 24th to the night of October 3rd, I had in all eight hours of sleep... We had no blankets, greatcoats, or waterproof sheets, nor any time or material to build new shelters. The rain poured down. Every night we went out to fetch in the dead... After the first day or two the corpses swelled and stank. I vomited more than once while superintending the carrying... The colour of the dead faces changed from white to yellow-grey...'.
Robert Graves, in 1916 from *Goodbye to All That*

Women making artillery shells in a munitions factory in Birmingham.

Rats infested the trenches and diseases spread among the men.

Back in Britain, the war brought about dramatic changes in family life. Most of the men were away at the Front, so that women had to take on many essential jobs. They worked in factories making weapons and ammunition, in coalfields, on farms and in the police and postal services. In fact, they did almost all of the jobs that men had done before the war. The main difference was that women were paid less than men had received for the same work. Even children were expected to 'do their bit', carrying messages, visiting wounded soldiers, doing farm work and collecting things that were useful for the war effort, including wool, rags and silver paper.

Some women welcomed the changes, as they gave them independence and an income. But for most the work was back-breaking. Munitions workers laboured for 12 hours at a time, often in dangerous conditions. Handling explosives gave many of the women a disease that turned their skin yellow. They became known as 'canary girls': 'skin tanned a yellow-brown, even to the roots of their hair, by the awful stuff they handled.' Besides working in industry, women also cared for the wounded. Some women went to France to work as

> During the War there was a feeling in Britain that all healthy young men, whatever their convictions, should volunteer to fight for their country. If they did not do so they were considered cowards.
>
> 'Yesterday afternoon, every lawn tennis court... was crowded by strapping young Englishmen... Is there no way of shaming these laggards? The English girl who will not know the man – lover, brother, friend – that cannot show an overwhelming reason for not taking up arms – that girl will do her duty and will give good help to her country.'
> Letter in *The Times*, August 1914

'I had a friend across the road, and I went to her birthday party. Her soldier father was on leave at the time, and we sat in a ring round his feet playing 'Simon Says'. He went back to France the next day. Not long after, I saw an envelope being delivered to the house; he had been killed in a German artillery bombardment. He was never found and, until the day she died, my friend's mother believed he was wandering about somewhere in France suffering from loss of memory.'

Recollections of a woman who was 8 years old in 1916.

Children marching in London, 1915.

nurses. 'In 1917 I joined the VADS... we had to go out at night to meet the trains bringing the wounded... next morning two of us would attend the burials – I can never forget those lines of coffins,' wrote a volunteer nurse.

In addition to their 'war work', married women also had to look after their families. Many foods became scarce and expensive, and it was sometimes difficult to get enough to eat. On top of all their hardships, people at home were constantly worried about the men who were away fighting. All families, rich and poor, lived in constant dread of the telegram telling them of the death of a husband, father, son or brother.

Sad partings at Victoria Station, London, as soldiers leave for the front.

3 BETWEEN THE WARS

Unemployed men queueing to collect their 'dole' in the 1930s.

When the First World War ended in 1918, many people hoped that their lives would return to normal. Despite their hard work during the war, women were expected to give up their jobs in industry to men coming home from the armed forces. Having gained some independence, many women were reluctant to lose it. But in the end they had no choice. Even so, the men found that there were simply not enough jobs for them. The situation was to become even worse as businesses collapsed, prices rose and wages fell. In June 1921 more than two million people were unemployed; in 1932 the figure had risen to almost three million.

The government paid unemployment benefit, or 'dole', to some people who were out of work, but it was so little that many families were living in a state of extreme poverty, especially in industrial areas. Even those who had work found that their wages were little better than the dole.

> In 1933 the Government introduced the Means Test, which meant that any money earned by a family was deducted from their dole.
>
> *'My wife was able to earn a few shillings to supplement our dole income...The final blow came when the Means Test was put into operation...Both my wife and son, who had just commenced to earn a few shillings, told me to get out, as I was living on them and taking the food they needed.'*
>
> Unemployed man in 1934

With so little money, many families could not afford to eat properly, and much of the food that was bought went to the man of the household, to keep him healthy enough to work. Women, particularly, suffered great hardships, especially if they had large families. They worked hard in the home and often went hungry. Meanwhile the old, terraced houses of the poor deteriorated into slums.

As the dole queues lengthened, the number of people who applied for each vacant job also increased. Hundreds of men would gather at the gates of a factory if there was even a rumour of an available job.

One man wrote of the effects of unemployment: 'You fall into the habit of slouching... of glancing at people furtively, ashamed of your secret...'.

Some men left their homes and families to set off, on foot, in search of work in other parts of the country. Others banded together and marched to London in protest against their unemployment and poverty.

Away from the main industrial areas, people were less affected by poverty. In the south of

Even in the 1930s, many poor houses had no running water.

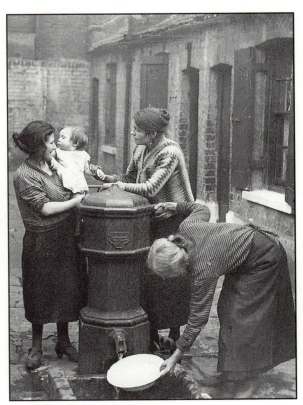

The smoking chimneys of a large cotton mill rise above the busy industrial town of Preston, Lancashire, in 1925.

Marchers on the Jarrow Crusade of 1936, protesting against unemployment.

England, new 'light' industries were being started. Council housing estates were built and, although far from luxurious, the houses did at least have plumbing and electricity. Among the middle and upper classes, there seemed little hardship, other than a shortage of servants.

At about this time new labour-saving appliances were becoming available in the shops. Vacuum cleaners, electric ovens, refrigerators and washing machines were all eagerly bought by middle-class women.

> 'Mrs J... had "gone away almost to a skeleton" through sheer starvation. Though she was nursing her baby, I found that all the food she had yesterday was a cup of tea at breakfast-time, and tea and two slices of bread and butter... at tea-time... From the husband's unemployment pay of £1.5s a week had to go to pay off a debt, 6s 3d for rent, and only 8s 9d was left for food and fire. A school dinner for the eldest child was divided with his brother and saved them from utter starvation...'.
>
> Quoted from *Life in Britain between the Wars* by L.C.B. Seamen

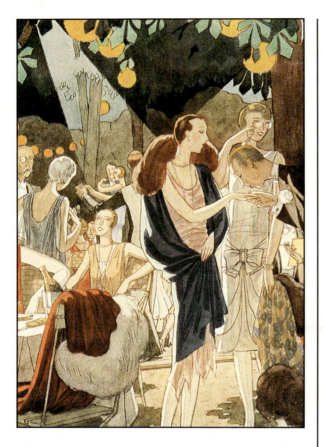

A group of wealthy and sophisticated young people enjoying themselves at a elegant party in the 'roaring twenties'.

> '[Miss Ponsonby] would, on an impulse, arrange a last-minute party and ask her friends to contribute an essential ingredient: some benevolent godfather would supply a band, other guests provided supper, all brought champagne...They had a splendid zest for life and ability for expressing that zest. Friends provided impromptu cabarets...elaborate and ingenious treasure hunts were arranged...and almost every night there was some excuse for putting on fancy dress.'
> From *The Glass of Fashion*
> (by Cecil Beaton)

Also popular were radios, or 'wireless' sets. Radio programmes were first broadcast in Britain in 1922, and by 1924 they could be heard in most parts of the country. Families gathered around the wireless to listen to the news, sports events, stories, music and other entertainment programmes, and 'Children's Hour'.

For young people with money, the years following the war were the 'roaring twenties'. Not for them the horrors of unemployment. They enjoyed themselves at parties and the theatre, visited the cinema and listened and danced to the new jazz music from America. Energetic dances such as the black-bottom and the charleston replaced the more sedate waltzes and foxtrots, and girls shocked their elders by wearing 'flapper dresses' that finished above the knee instead of below the ankle.

4   THE SECOND WORLD WAR

In 1939, Britain was at war once more. Again men were sent away to fight – not only in Europe but in North Africa, the Middle East and Asia, and on all of the world's oceans. Some women went with them, in 'auxiliary' or supporting roles, but most remained at home. As more and more men were conscripted into the armed services, women had to fill their jobs. Those without children were drafted into the women's sections of the armed forces or else worked in some kind of

Children are led into an air-raid shelter to protect them from bombs, 1940.

When bombs fell on British cities, countless homes were destroyed and many people were killed.

essential job such as in an armaments factory or as a teacher.

As in the 1914–18 war women took on many of the jobs previously done by men. They worked in factories and on railways, swept chimneys, repaired houses and delivered milk and mail. Women working in civil defence had some of the most dangerous jobs. They acted as air-raid wardens, firefighters, ambulance drivers and rescue workers. More than 80,000 others joined the Women's Land Army and helped to produce food. Despite their efforts, food was often in short supply and many items were rationed. 'The ration of food is terrible. Nearly everything has gone up to an awful lot of money. In one part of the country they have no soap' (Vera, aged 8).

Unlike during the First World War, large parts of the country were at risk from attack. Weapons had become much more powerful since 1918 and could be used over greater

> 'I remember that labels with our names on were pinned to our clothes before we left London. The labels frightened me as much as the idea of leaving my parents... Each morning my sister and I would leave home with our packed sandwiches and clothes. We would say goodbye to our parents. Our labels were pinned on and I felt sick. We were not told the date of the real departure in case the Germans bombed the train... So we had to leave home without knowing if we would return that day or not.'
> Mel Calman, recalling how it felt to be an evacuee from *Children in Wartime*, 1989

Children being evacuated from London to the safety of the countryside in 1940.

distances. Air raids by enemy planes and so-called 'flying bombs' meant that people living in cities and industrial areas were often in danger. Many city children were evacuated to the countryside where they would be safer. They went to live with local families, while their mothers remained in the cities. In this way, many families were split up.

Throughout the war, children continued to go to school. If their parents were wealthy they might be sent to a fee-paying boarding school. Middle-class children would probably go to a primary school until they were 11 years old, and then to a grammar or secondary modern school.

In spite of a call by the British Youth Peace Assembly in 1940 that 'the school-leaving age should be re-constituted to provide for the school-leaving age to 15', many children of poor parents finished their education at the age of 11 years.

In 1944 a new Education Act was passed by Parliament. It stated that all children in Britain had to go to school until they were 15, and that their education was to be provided free.

'I drove an ambulance in London during the Blitz. It was terribly hard to drive, not like vehicles today. I had to go out and pick up people wounded in the air raids. It was pitch black at night because of the blackout; no one was allowed to leave any light showing in case it helped the German bombers. Often the only light came from buildings that were on fire. My husband, Bert, was away in the Navy. We'd only been married a few months when war broke out and I missed him. But there was a great feeling that everyone was working together, fighting for the same cause, and that helped a lot.'

Kathleen, a woman ambulance driver from 1940–44

'Everything I have is gone. Not that I mind – I'm alive, and that's all that matters. My husband scoffed at me for running into the street shelters. He said "fancy running out like that. Stay indoors." But I wouldn't listen to him. Good job too – else where would I be?... Everything I have ever worked for – it took me 15 years to build it up and look at it now. Nothing left at all. Still, we can always find another home. Thank goodness we're alive.'

Quoted from *The Blitz* (Mass Observation Archive, 1987)

Right *A London family in 1940 sharing a meal with their neighbours, whose home across the street has been bombed.*

22

5 A CHANGING WORLD

The years immediately after the end of the Second World War in 1945 were a time of austerity. There was a shortage of houses, fuel and food. But during the fifties Britain became steadily more prosperous. Most workers had jobs, and wages were fairly high. As a result, many families were able to buy goods that they could not have afforded previously, including labour-saving household appliances such as washing machines and vacuum cleaners, as well as 'luxury' items like televisions and even cars.

The working week was also becoming shorter and holidays longer, which gave people more time to spend on leisure. Many families took their first ever holidays away from home – a week or two at one of the new holiday camps. Foreign holidays were still limited to the rich, but in the sixties, air travel became cheaper, enabling many working families to go on 'package' holidays to resorts in Europe.

A 1950s teenager shows off some of his possessions, including a television.

The popularity of television increased rapidly. Within a few years it became the major form of family entertainment. As more and more people discovered the pleasures of being able to watch programmes in their own home, the popularity of the cinema declined.

People's general health improved during the fifties and sixties. This was partly because of advances in medicine, including immunization against major infectious diseases. It was also due to the National Health Service (NHS) which had been created in the late 1940s.

During the 1950s, Butlin's camps provided affordable family holidays.

For the first time all men, women and children could obtain free medical and dental treatment.

Housing also improved during this period, as war-damaged streets and decaying slums were torn down to make way for new estates. Unfortunately, many were replaced by 'high-rise' blocks of flats, in which many families felt isolated from the rest of the community, causing housing and social problems for later decades.

Fifties mothers were under a great deal of pressure to devote themselves to looking after their children and home rather than going out to work. In turn, children were expected to develop into young adults – with the same interests and beliefs as their parents, and the same taste in music and clothes – and most young adults lived at home with their parents until they got married.

All this was to change with the arrival of 'youth culture'. In a movement that began in the fifties with rock'n'roll and continued to accelerate throughout the sixties, young people adopted new styles of music, dress and behaviour that set them apart from their elders.

Dear Janice,
Living in London is absolutely fab! I'm sharing a flat with Liz, Sue and Mandy, and we're having a great time going to parties and concerts. I've got a job in a boutique in Carnaby Street; it doesn't pay much but it's enough to live on and I get a discount on clothes. Sometimes pop stars come into the shop – I'm waiting for one of them to invite me to a party! We're having our own party in the flat soon. Why don't you come down for it? When you've seen London you'll never want to go back home again...'

From a letter written by 16-year-old Sarah to a friend in 1968

In the 1950s, coffee bars became popular places for teenagers to meet, talk and listen to music.

After the end of the Second World War, there was a great increase in the number of families coming to Britain from Commonwealth countries. They were encouraged by offers of work in the NHS, in public transport, and in other jobs that were difficult to fill. Some Britons found it hard to accept these immigrants and subjected them to prejudice and abuse. Black families searching for jobs or places to live often came up against the 'colour bar'. This type of racial discrimination was not outlawed until 1968.

Families from the Caribbean island of Jamaica arriving in Britain to begin a new life in 1958.

'When we arrived at Waterloo Station we were met by a group of students, all waving placards with 'Welcome Commonwealth Citizens' and 'Good Luck'. We didn't realize how much luck we would need until we started looking for a place to live. I walked along miles of streets, looking for 'Room to Rent' signs in the windows. When I knocked on doors asking about the rooms, most landladies just looked me up and down and said the rooms were taken. Some said that they didn't rent to 'coloured' people. Some even specified 'No Coloureds' on their sign.'

An immigrant worker from Jamaica on arrival in London in 1959

6 THE SEVENTIES ONWARDS

Early in the seventies the Western world was hit by an oil crisis. As this vital commodity became scarce and expensive, companies went out of business and unemployment increased sharply. Prices also rose throughout the decade, which further added to the problems of the unemployed. When a new government came to power in 1979, inflation was reduced but only at the expense of soaring unemployment: from 1.3 million in 1979 to over 3 million in 1983. As in past decades, the industrial areas and the inner-cities were worst hit. After a brief drop, both inflation and unemployment started to rise again.

The seventies and, especially, the eighties saw society becoming increasingly divided between the 'haves' and the 'have-nots'. Although many people found themselves better off, the poor and those without work suffered. The number of people who owned (rather than rented) their own homes rose; so did the number of those who had no home at all.

London and some other cities had large homeless populations, often consisting mainly of young people who felt they had no prospects in their home towns and had come to the cities to find work. Sometimes they built their own cities-within-cities, making 'houses' from cardboard

Two 'modern' kitchens, one in a wealthy suburban home and the other in a slum.

A homeless man sleeping on a city street in 1990.

'What's the point of staying on at school? There aren't any jobs so why waste time studying for more exams? My brother Tony stayed on and look where it got him – into the dole queue. If you ask me I might as well leave now and sign on as soon as I can. At least I'll get some money.'

Interview with Tracey aged 15, March 1982

boxes and other discarded materials.

The ties that held families together were becoming looser. On the one hand fewer couples got married and, on the other, new laws made it easier to get divorced. Many husbands and wives who had been trapped in unhappy marriages were able to part. As a result, the number of one-parent families increased; the majority of single parents were women.

This young man is a single parent and is bringing up his child on his own.

Young men, women and children demonstrate against nuclear weapons in 1986.

'I left home in Lancashire because there didn't seem to be anything going for me there. London was the place, I thought – jobs, money, excitement, you name it. My money didn't last long; I thought I'd soon get a job but it didn't work out. I can't afford to pay rent so I sleep in doorways, under bridges, in parks – anywhere I can find. I can't get anywhere permanent to live until I find a job, and I can't get a job unless I've got somewhere to live. I can't even claim the dole unless I go back home. There's nothing I can do except beg for money and tell myself things will get better.'
Interview with Steve, aged 22, who left Salford in 1989

In most homes, television remained the most important form of entertainment, watched by millions. The youth culture that had been so prominent in the sixties did not disappear. It became more varied and less provocative; in general, young people were rather less rebellious towards their parents than they had been earlier.

The most popular home entertainment.

IMPORTANT DATES

1901 Queen Victoria's death. King Edward VII comes to the throne.
1906 Education authorities to provide meals for poor children.
1908 Seperate juvenile courts established.
1909 Introduction of labour exchanges in Britain.
1914–18 First World War.
1918 Women over 30 allowed to vote. Education Act raising school leaving age to 14.
1921 First birth control centre in England opened in London.
1922 British Broadcasting Co. (later BBC) make first regular broadcasts.
1925 Pensions Act, providing old age pensions and pensions for widows and orphans.
1928 Women allowed to vote on the same terms as men.
1932 Children and Young Persons Act reformed juvenile court procedure.
1936 First TV broadcasts from Alexandra Palace, London.
1939–45 Second World War.
1940 Introduction of food rationing in Britain.
1944 Education Act passed, raising the school leaving age to 15.
1967 Abortion Act permitted termination of pregnancy on the recommendation of two doctors.
1968 Race Relations Act.
1969 Voting age for men and women reduced from 21 to 18. Family Law Reform Act lowered coming of age to 18. Divorce Reform Act.
1970 Equal Pay Act.
1976 Sex Discrimination Act.

PICTURE ACKNOWLEDGEMENTS

ET Archives cover; Mary Evans Picture Library 8 (both), 9, 13 (both), 14, 16, 17, 18, 21; Mansell Collection 12; Peter Newark Pictures 22; Topham Picture Library 4, 6, 7, 15, 19, 20, 23, 24, 25, 26, 27 (left), 28 (top), 29; Wayland Picture Library 5 (both), 10, 11, 27 (right), 28, 29.

GLOSSARY

Austerity When consumer goods and luxuries are in short supply.
Blitz The heavy bombing of London by German planes during the Second World War
Boutique Another name for a shop. It was first used in the sixties to describe clothing shops that catered for youth fashions.
Breadwinner Someone who earns money for a family.
Conscripted Ordered to join the armed forces.
Divorce When a marriage is ended legally.
Dole (unemployment benefit) Money paid by a government to people who are out of work.
Evacuation Moving people out of an area, usually in time of danger or following a disaster, such as severe flooding.
Front In war, the area in which opposing armies do battle.
Immunization Protecting people from a disease, usually by an injection.
Inflation A measure of how fast the prices of goods rise.
Munitions workers People who work in factories where weapons and ammunition are made.
One-parent family A family in which the children are brought up by just one of their parents.
Package holiday A type of holiday in which the transport and accommodation are arranged by the holiday company and are included in the price of the holiday.
Penny Represented by the letter 'd', it was a unit of currency equivalent to two-hundred-and-fortieth of a pound. The penny disappeared in 1970 when decimal currency was introduced.
Shilling Represented by the letter 's' it was a unit of English currency equivalent to one-twentieth of a pound until replaced by the 5p piece in 1970.
Sophisticated Fashionable.
VADS Volunteer nurses in the Voluntary Aid Detachment.

BOOKS TO READ

Britain Since 1945 by Nigel Smith (Wayland, 1990)
English Life in the First World War by Christopher Martin (Wayland, 1974)
The Forties and Fifties by Nathaniel Harris (Macdonald, 1975)
How We Used to Live, 1902-1926 by Freda Kelsall (A & C Black, 1985)
How We Used to Live, 1954-1970 by Freda Kelsall (A & C Black, 1987)
The Sixties by Nathaniel Harris (Macdonald, 1975)
Women and the Family by Kate Hyndley (Wayland, 1989)
Women and War by A. Susan Williams (Wayland, 1989)

INDEX

air raids 21
air raid shelter 19
austerity 23

bombing 20, 22
British Empire 6
broadcasting 18
business collapse 14

'canary girls' 12, 2
'cardboard cities' 28
children's war effort 12
cinemas 10, 24
coffee bars 25

demonstrations 29
divorce 15
dole queues 14, 15

entertainment 5, 10
evacuation 20, 21

factories 6, 7, 8, 9, 12, 20
factory owners 9
factory workers 7, 9
First World War 11–13
flying bombs 21
food shortage 23

foreign holidays 23
fuel shortage 23

gramophone 10

holiday camps 23, 24
homeless people 27, 28
houses 6, 7, 9, 15, 23, 25
   council estates 17
   slum housing (see slums)
   wealthy 9, 8
   workers' 6, 7

immigrants 26
inflation 27

Jarrow March 17

labour-saving
   appliances 17, 23

middle classes 9, 9–10, 18, 21

National Health Service 24

oil crisis 28

poverty 4, 7, 8, 14–15

racial discrimination 26
radios 18
recreation 8, 23
rock 'n' roll 25
'roaring twenties' 18

sanitation 6, 15
schools 21
school leaving age 21, 22
Second World War 19–22
servants 9, 10, 17
slums 15, 25

television 7, 23, 24, 29

unemployment 8, 14, 15, 17, 18, 27
unemployment benefit (dole) 14

women at the Front 13
women in war work 9, 11, 18–19, 20, 21
Womens Land Army 20

youth culture 25

ACKNOWLEDGEMENTS

Quotations on the following pages are reprinted by kind permission of; Virago Press from *A Testament of Youth* by Vera Brittain page 10, Weidenfeld and Nicolson from *The Glass of Fashion* by Cecil Beaton page 18.